Alive in the WORD

SEASONS OF OUR LIVES

FROM HOME TO HOME

Finding Meaning in Mobility

Justin Huyck

Little Rock Scripture Study

A ministry of the Diocese of Little Rock in partnership with Liturgical Press

Nihil obstat: Jerome Kodell, OSB, *Censor Librorum.*
Imprimatur: ✠ Anthony B. Taylor, Bishop of Little Rock, May 4, 2018.

Cover design by Ann Blattner. Cover photo: Getty Images. Used with permission.

Photos/illustrations: Pages 6, 15, 19, 24, 27, 28, 30, 34, 38, 41, 45, 46, Getty Images. Used with permission. Pages 9, 22, 39, Clifford M. Yeary.

 Published by Liturgical Press, Collegeville, Minnesota 56321. Printed in the United States of America.

ISBN: 978-0-8146-4404-1 (print); 978-0-8146-4429-4 (e-book)

Contents

Introduction

Alive in the Word brings you resources to deepen your understanding of Scripture, offer meaning for your life today, and help you to pray and act in response to God's word.

Use any volume of **Alive in the Word** in the way best suited to you.

- **For individual learning and reflection**, consider this an invitation to prayerfully journal in response to the questions you find along the way. And be prepared to move from head to heart and then to action.
- **For group learning and reflection**, arrange for three sessions where you will use the material provided as the basis for faith sharing and prayer. You may ask group members to read each chapter in advance and come prepared with questions answered. In this kind of session, plan to be together for about an hour. Or, if your group prefers, read and respond to the questions together without advance preparation. With this approach, it's helpful to plan on spending more time for each group session

in order to adequately work through each of the chapters.

- **For a parish-wide event or use within a larger group,** provide each person with a copy of this volume, and allow time during the event for quiet reading, group discussion and prayer, and then a final commitment by each person to some simple action in response to what he or she learned.

This volume on the topic of mobility is one of several volumes that explore **Seasons of Our Lives.** While the Scriptures remain constant, we have the opportunity to find within them a fresh message as we go through life facing various challenges. Whether the circumstances in our lives change due to our own decisions or due to the natural process of aging and maturing, we bring with us the actual lived experiences of this world to our prayerful reading of the Bible. This series provides an opportunity to acknowledge our own circumstances and to find how God continues to work in us through changing times.

Mobility and Vocation

Begin by quietly asking God to assist you in your prayer and study. Then read Genesis 11:31–12:9, one of the early stories of God's calling forth people to move to the unknown.

Genesis 11:31–12:9
31Terah took his son Abram, his grandson Lot, son of Haran,
and his daughter-in-law Sarai, the wife of his son Abram, and
brought them out of Ur of the Chaldeans, to go to the land
of Canaan. But when they reached Haran, they settled there.
32The lifetime of Terah was two hundred and five years; then
Terah died in Haran.

1The LORD said to Abram: Go forth from your land, your
relatives, and from your father's house to a land that I will
show you. 2I will make of you a great nation, and I will bless
you; I will make your name great, so that you will be a blessing.
3I will bless those who bless you and curse those who curse
you. All the families of the earth will find blessing in you.

4 Abram went as the LORD directed him, and
Lot went with him. Abram was seventy-five years
old when he left Haran. 5 Abram took his wife
Sarai, his brother's son Lot, all the possessions
that they had accumulated, and the persons they
had acquired in Haran, and they set out for the
land of Canaan. When they came to the land of
Canaan, 6 Abram passed through the land as far
as the sacred place at Shechem, by the oak of
Moreh. The Canaanites were then in the land.
7 The LORD appeared to Abram and said: To
your descendants I will give this land. So Abram
built an altar there to the LORD who had ap-
peared to him. 8 From there he moved on to the
hill country east of Bethel, pitching his tent with
Bethel to the west and Ai to the east. He built
an altar there to the LORD and invoked the LORD
by name. 9 Then Abram journeyed on by stages
to the Negeb.

Following a few moments of quiet reflection on the passage, consider the background information provided in "Setting the Scene."

Setting the Scene

The experience of moving, or moving again and again, can have a profound impact on one's sense of identity. For some, it may be difficult to see beyond the immediate transitions and the reasons for them and to discern a larger arc to one's life. Reflecting on the ancient story of Abram and Sarai can help people today see our own experiences of geographic mobility as graced and formative dimensions of our life stories. Moreover, through the story of Abram and Sarai (later known as Abraham and Sarah), we might consider how our stories of mobility are sacred vocation stories, with significance beyond our own lives, woven into God's story of creation and care for the entire human family.

This passage comes shortly after a group of stories in the first eleven chapters of the book of Genesis, which are narrative reflections on the origins and identity of humanity in general. These include the well-known accounts of creation, Adam and Eve, Cain and Abel, Noah and the Flood, and the Tower of Babel. Now, we are introduced to the origins and identity of Israel in particular through its various patriarchs and ancestors. In this first introduction to Abram and Sarai, we already begin to see that Israel's story is one of mobility.

Indeed, some of the earliest hearers of this story encountered it out of their own experience of mobility, during and after the time of the Babylonian exile (597–538 BCE), when much of the Judean population was forced to leave their land in the wake of the fall of Jerusalem (587). It was during and after the exile that these stories in Genesis and in the wider Pentateuch (the Bible's first five books) were edited and collected. It was a time of questioning and uncertainty about national identity. Our ancestors in faith found meaning for themselves in Abram and Sarai's mobility and so can we.

The passage from Genesis 11:31–12:9 will be considered a few verses at a time. The questions that appear occasionally in the margins are for group discussion or personal reflection.

Understanding the Scene Itself

31Terah took his son Abram, his grandson Lot, son of Haran, and his daughter-in-law Sarai, the wife of his son Abram, and brought them out of Ur of the Chaldeans, to go to the land of Canaan. But when they reached Haran, they settled there. 32The lifetime of Terah was two hundred and five years; then Terah died in Haran.

For Abram, the city of Haran and its surrounding region is an important place in his life story. In some ways, this city in northern Mesopotamia is an unexpected home, the result of Abram's father Terah's uprooting his family (including Abram and his wife Sarai) from his native land in Ur, in southern Mesopotamia. Terah's intention in leaving Ur seems to have been to travel to Canaan, but for some reason the family settles in Haran. Abram and Sarai will eventually make the trip down to Canaan after Terah's death but, in the meantime, the lengthy settlement in Haran has an important formative

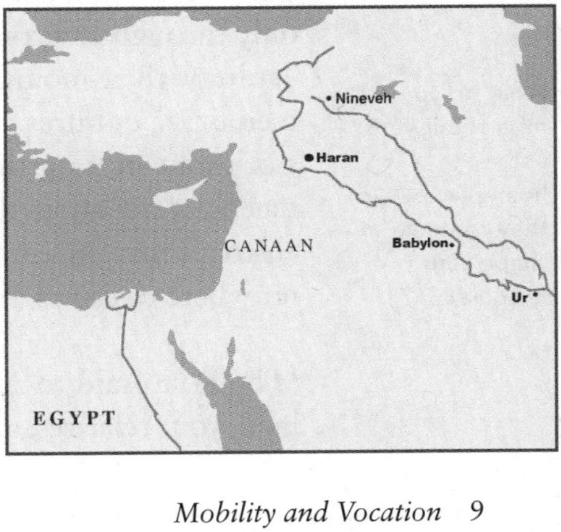

impact—not only on Abram and Sarai, but on their eventual family.

For Abram and his family, Haran is not their initial homeland, but it will continue to be a place that grounds their identity, even after that identity shifts to the new land of Canaan. Years later, we will hear how Abram insists on following the ancient practice of endogamy (arranging marriages within one's own tribe) by procuring his son Isaac's wife (Rebekah) from his family in the same region surrounding Haran, in nearby Nahor (Gen 24:3, 10). Likewise, Isaac's wife, Rebekah, will encourage Isaac to send *their* son, Jacob, to Haran, ostensibly to procure wives, which he does in Leah and Rachel (Gen 27:43; 28:10).

Name and reflect on the place(s) that formed you in your childhood or youth: How were you shaped by their geography, cultures, institutions, or pace of life?

In the face of mobility, we too may find ourselves returning to the places that formed us, even if only in our hearts. Our homelands have shaped us, and may continue to capture our imaginations, in various ways. Often, our places of origin formed us through their geography: the mountains that surrounded us, the rivers that meandered through our lives, the plains that expanded our vision. Ultimately, though, places form us not only through environment, but through a wider ecology that includes community practices, memories, cultures, institutions, networks, and stories. Even if our homeland's life patterns are much different than those of patriarchal marriage customs, they have no less a hold on us—no matter where our lives may take us.

What do you miss about your early homeplaces? Do they continue to shape your imagination?

[1]The LORD said to Abram: Go forth from your land, your relatives, and from your father's house

to a land that I will show you. [2]I will make of you a great nation, and I will bless you; I will make your name great, so that you will be a blessing. [3]I will bless those who bless you and curse those who curse you. All the families of the earth will find blessing in you.

One of the significant aspects of the Abram story is God's intimate involvement in companioning him through his mobility. God's companionship begins with his call to Abram here, and continues in subsequent promises (e.g., Gen 15; Gen 18; Gen 22). But lest we think that intimacy always means comfort, we are struck by the deeply disturbing nature of God's call to Abram, "Go forth from your land" (v. 1), which would seem to be unwelcome to someone who had been settled in Haran for some time.

What words or phrases would you use to describe "going forth" from home or another place that was important to you?

As we have seen, Abram's identity was deeply connected to the region of Haran and his family that lived there—and would continue to be even after his departure. And yet, God calls him to "go forth" from his homeland to a new land. For those who live mobility today, the experience of moving to new places may be just as unsettling and identity-rattling, whether it is mixed with excitement, fear, or despair. Abram would hardly be encouraged by the first of the promises that follow: to make of Abram a "great nation" (v. 2). After all, one of the important points of the genealogy that precedes this account (Gen 11:30) is that Abram's wife, Sarai, is barren. How can God fulfill this promise?

Called by God
Called as we are
Called from
a place or
situation

How is Abram to make sense of this call and his impending mobility?

In *The Stories We Live*, theologian Kathleen Cahalan describes vocation in ways that might resonate with both Abram's initial call and how we experience mobility today. Cahalan suggests that vocation is multidimensional, and she describes these various dimensions of vocation through a series of prepositions. For example, Cahalan notes that we are called *by* God in multiple ways, *as* we are, and *from* our particular places and situations. In Abram, we can recognize such an experience that leaves room for human action and creativity on Abram's part. Likewise, Abram is called *as* he and Sarai *are*—even if her barrenness might seem counterintuitive to God's promise for a great nation. Finally, and most harrowingly, God calls Abram to go forth *from* the land that has given him an identity. "To be called *from* entails moving away, an ending, before a new beginning is clear. . . . It requires you to trust that moving away is the right path, a calling, even though you do not know the destination" (Cahalan, *The Stories We Live: Finding God's Calling All around Us*). Embracing this sense of vocation may help us live mobility today with *faith* that God really does call us as we are, from one place to an uncertain future, but also with *hope* about the possibilities for our future journeying—that vocation

If you have moved, did you feel ready to move to a new place? Can you look back now and see that "God called you as you were"?

involves both God's companionship as well as freedom for our creativity.

Moreover, the promises made to Abram in this passage suggest that an embrace of mobility in his vocation would be a blessing not only for him and his family, but would have implications for others: that God would return the blessings and curses heaped on Abram by others and that "all the families of the earth" would find blessing in him (v. 3). Such promises reflect Abram's rootedness in the wider human story, as previously noted, and may also reflect later interactions as he made his move through Canaan (Gen 14:18; Gen 20:7, 17). In any case, for those living mobility today, we might recognize a challenge to be attentive to others as we move from known to unknown places, recognizing God's intimate presence in others' lives as well as our own. We might also reflect on the impact our mobility can have on the lives of others, as we will continue to explore in the next section.

[4]Abram went as the LORD directed him, and Lot went with him. Abram was seventy-five years old when he left Haran. [5]Abram took his wife Sarai, his brother's son Lot, all the possessions that they had accumulated, and the persons they had acquired in Haran, and they set out for the land of Canaan.

In this first encounter with God, Abram responds without hesitation to the path placed before him. In later encounters, Abram and Sarai will respond with incredulity and even laughter to God's continued promise of progeny (Gen 15; Gen 18). But here, directed to leave his land, Abram does so without question or response. Just as Noah had earlier responded to his vocation to build an ark in service of humanity's future (Gen 6:14-22), so too Abram responds to his vocation of mobility and in so doing provides hope for humanity's continued journeying. We might consider how our acceptance of mobility is also an act of faith that God works through us, wherever we might go.

How has your experience of mobility had a positive impact on someone else's life?

Abram does not leave his land empty-handed, for he and Sarai bring with them all the possessions and people he has accumulated in Haran (v. 5). This passage depicts him as a wealthy man, who has found great success in Haran—and yet is willing to depart anyway. Perhaps this is one of the greatest challenges of mobility, to leave behind places that have been quite fruitful for us—whether that fruitfulness is in wealth or, as is often the case, friendships and experiences, career skills and competencies. Like Abram, we carry as much of what we have accumulated as we can in our move to the next place.

What have you "accumulated" from past places where you have lived? What experiences, memories, or skills do you continue to value today?

When they came to the land of Canaan,
[6]Abram passed through the land as far as the sacred place at Shechem, by the oak of Moreh. The Canaanites were then in the land.

[7]The Lord appeared to Abram and said: To your descendants I will give this land. So Abram built an altar there to the Lord who had appeared to him.
[8]From there he moved on to the hill country east of Bethel, pitching his tent with

Bethel to the west and Ai to the east. He built an altar there to the LORD and invoked the LORD by name. [9]Then Abram journeyed on by stages to the Negeb.

As Abram enters into Canaan, it is clear that his journeying is not complete, for he moves through Canaan, with stops in Shechem (v. 6), the region around Bethel (v. 8), and then continuing south by stages to the Negeb (v. 9). This presages the chapters to come that will chronicle Abraham, Isaac, and Jacob's continuing mobility throughout Canaan, Egypt, and Haran (Gen 12–37), as well as Israel's continued migration into and then bondage in Egypt (Gen 37–50; Exod 1–12), the dramatic climax of its exodus of Egypt (Exod 13–15), and the stories of migration back to Canaan in the biblical books that follow. In the contemporary world as well, moving is often experienced as an ongoing process of planning, packing, making various arrangements, traveling, unpacking (or not unpacking!). Sometimes it seems, like Abram, we are never quite "settled"!

As Abram moves about this new land, his process includes discovering its particular features and their significance to the local people. Thus, in the city of Shechem he discovers the oak of Moreh that, like many natural features in the ancient world, is imbued with sacred significance and recognized as a shrine (v. 6). This recognition is an example of the distinction that many have made between "place" and "space." In today's globalized world, the particular flavor of local *places* has sometimes given way to a "flattening" of *space*, to the extent that our spaces (malls, office buildings, even churches) may not provide any sense of locality. Abram's experience in Shechem can be a reminder to reflect on the particular stories and significance of the new places we inhabit in our mobility, taking time to discover local historical sites and buildings, neighborhoods and their backstories, culinary habits and community practices.

What are the buildings, stories, or customs you have found significant in new places?

And yet, Abram also retains his own practices and values, even as he explores this new place. While the shrine at Shechem may have its own particular history and meaning, his encounter of God there (v. 7) is nevertheless shaped by his *own* narrative, his own past experiences with God. At this new sacred place, as in his homeland in Haran, he recognizes again that his vocation will include the gift of land and descendants. His building of an altar in this place, as well as in the hill country outside Bethel (v. 8), is a recognition that both God's presence and Abram's vocation endure in this new land. Abram is marking this new place as holy for him, where he can live the identity formed in him from his homeland and yet also be open to how that identity will be colored, stretched, and transformed in this new land.

In *The Land: Place as Gift, Promise, and Challenge in Biblical Faith*, Scripture scholar Walter Brueggemann writes that "place is space in which important words have been spoken which have established identity, defined vocation, and envisioned destiny." Sometimes, we may seem like an outsider in our new places, just as Abram camped just outside Bethel. Nevertheless, Abram's story can encourage us to be "at home" with our mobility, attentive to God's presence and the shaping of our vocation and identity, in sometimes surprising ways and in unlikely places.

How has your identify and vocation been shaped because of your mobility, in new places or surprising ways?

Praying the Word / Sacred Reading

Formed and shaped from dirt and water,
Forged in love from earth's debris.
God's own life now flowing through us,
God's own breath our energy.
Life and death can never stain us,
Through the ash, God's love we see.

Formed and fed by bread from heaven,
Fed, sustained by hearty Word.
Ever-present in our wanderings,
God now tasted, seen, and heard.
Life renewed, transformed, transfigured,
Mission's hope, a world restored.

(Prayers in this volume are adapted or taken from faithshape.org, the website of Justin Huyck.)

Living the Word

- *As we discover our vocations in the midst of mobility, it is important to develop spiritual practices that can help us reflect on God's continuing presence and companionship. Consider attending a retreat, perhaps rooted in the spirituality of St. Ignatius of Loyola, designed to help you reflect on your life's journey. Some retreat centers (and parishes) also have a labyrinth on site—a wonderful way to "walk" your prayer. (To find a labyrinth, go to labyrinthlocator.com.)*

- *Follow Abram's example of traveling through the land by getting to know your new home: subscribe to the local newspaper, visit its various neighborhoods, go for a hike in nearby parks and recreational areas, inquire about shrines or religious centers that celebrate local religious history (e.g., those related to local saints, leaders, or events).*

- *Encounter the diversity of your community by participating in service projects. Check with your parish or local agencies, including community centers for youth, homeless shelters, or hunger organizations. Seek out those that are not in your neighborhood: This is a great way to make a difference, and to learn more about your new home.*

Mobility and Family

Begin by quietly asking God to assist you in your prayer and study. Then read Matthew 2:13-23, the story of the Holy Family's escape to Egypt.

Matthew 2:13-23
13When [the magi] had departed, behold, the angel of the
Lord appeared to Joseph in a dream and said, "Rise, take the
child and his mother, flee to Egypt, and stay there until I tell
you. Herod is going to search for the child to destroy him."
14Joseph rose and took the child and his mother by night and
departed for Egypt. 15He stayed there until the death of Herod,
that what the Lord had said through the prophet might be
fulfilled, "Out of Egypt I called my son."

16When Herod realized that he had been deceived by the
magi, he became furious. He ordered the massacre of all the
boys in Bethlehem and its vicinity two years old and under,
in accordance with the time he had ascertained from the
magi. 17Then was fulfilled what had been said through Jere-
miah the prophet:

**18"A voice was heard in Ramah,
sobbing and loud lamentation;
Rachel weeping for her children,
and she would not be consoled,
since they were no more."**

**19When Herod had died, behold, the angel of the
Lord appeared in a dream to Joseph in Egypt
20and said, "Rise, take the child and his mother
and go to the land of Israel, for those who sought
the child's life are dead." 21He rose, took the
child and his mother, and went to the land of
Israel. 22But when he heard that Archelaus was
ruling over Judea in place of his father Herod,
he was afraid to go back there. And because he
had been warned in a dream, he departed for the
region of Galilee. 23He went and dwelt in a town
called Nazareth, so that what had been spoken
through the prophets might be fulfilled, "He
shall be called a Nazorean."**

> *After reading and reflecting a few moments on the passage from Matthew, read the background information provided in "Setting the Scene."*

Setting the Scene

Living away from extended families can mean being separated from familial traditions, gatherings, and practices. Often, family dispersion is experienced mutually throughout the extended family. Extended families can find themselves living in various parts of the country or world, straining family connections by limiting shared experiences. On the other hand, family dispersion can be an opportunity for individuals to grow and households to form in their own particular ways, maintaining shared practices and relationships while also weaving new experiences into a common family narrative.

In some ways, the connection of Jesus, Mary, and Joseph to Bethlehem may seem surprising. All four gospels suggest that Jesus grew up—not in the Judean city of Bethlehem—but in the insignificant town of Nazareth in the region of Galilee to the north (Matt 2:23 and 13:54; Mark 1:9 and 6:1; Luke 2:4 and 4:16; John 1:46). This seems to be the town of Mary (Luke 1:26-27) and the place where Joseph would settle with her and Jesus (Matt 2:23; Luke 2:39). Moreover, much of Jesus' ministry, especially his early ministry, will take place in the surrounding area of Galilee (e.g., Matt 4:12-25, explored later).

While it is clear that Jesus grew up in Nazareth, the gospels of Matthew and Luke begin with infancy narratives centered in Bethlehem. These accounts help us to connect the family of Jesus, Mary, and Joseph to a larger kinship story, since Bethlehem was also the birthplace for Jesus' ancestor King David (John 7:42). Just as David emerged from Bethlehem as a humble shepherd who would become king (1 Sam 16), so too Jesus is recognized as the one who would come from Bethlehem to shepherd the people of Israel (Matt 2:6). Indeed, it is magi, Gentile astrologers from the east, who make this observation, which reinforces what is already evident in the ancestry of Jesus (and David): The genealogy of Jesus (Matt 1:1-17) involves a myriad of stories, including those of Gentile "outsiders" (e.g., Ruth, David's great-grandmother) who have added various textures to this "family history." Of course, Jesus' place in this lineage adds one more texture, as he is recognized by Joseph as his son, even though conceived through the Holy Spirit (Matt 1:20-25). Thus, by making Bethlehem an early focal point, the gospels of Matthew and Luke are able to integrate the story of Jesus, Mary, and Joseph within a larger multi-textured kinship structure and narrative.

The Gospel of Matthew's account of Jesus' birth and the Holy Family's migration is particularly dramatic and harrowing. As it progresses, it moves from Bethlehem in a way that interweaves their experience with various dimensions, people, and places of Israel's larger story. By reflecting on it, we might consider how our own sense of family is stretched or enriched by the mobility we experience, even if our experiences offer a different type of drama. Thus, the Holy Family's displacement in Egypt can help us reflect on the impact of mobility and migration on contemporary families and family culture. Herod's massacre of the children in Bethlehem offers us a way to consider how we share family burdens across distance. Finally,

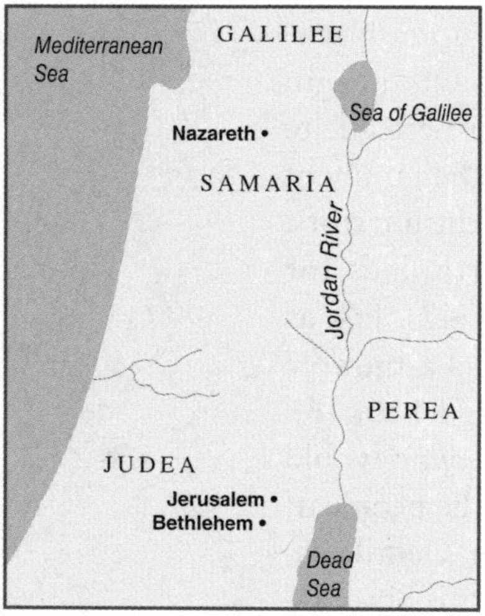

the Holy Family's settling in Nazareth can help us reflect on God's presence, wherever our families dwell.

The passage will now be examined a few verses at a time to allow for deeper understanding. Questions in the margin are for personal use or group discussion.

Understanding the Scene Itself

**13When [the magi] had departed, behold, the
angel of the Lord appeared to Joseph in a dream
and said, "Rise, take the child and his mother,
flee to Egypt, and stay there until I tell you.
Herod is going to search for the child to destroy
him." 14Joseph rose and took the child and his
mother by night and departed for Egypt. 15He
stayed there until the death of Herod, that what
the Lord had said through the prophet might be
fulfilled, "Out of Egypt I called my son."**

Families experience mobility for a wide variety of reasons. For some, mobility is an essential, and even exhilarating, component of career advancement, study, or professional training. For others, mobility is a sudden and traumatic experience after a lost job or a company reassignment. Military families typically experience frequent mobility as they move from base to base and country to country. Sometimes, mobility is an expression

of family care for a chronically ill spouse or child, as when a family relocates within proximity of needed medical care. Finally, mobility can be horrific for refugees fleeing violence, as Joseph, Mary, and Jesus do in this passage, and as so many families do today.

How has your experience of mobility shifted or affected "roles" in your family?

Whether exhilarating or excruciating, mobility tends to stretch a family's sense of identity, both in relationship to extended familial traditions (as introduced above) and also for the particular household. For example, moving from one place to another might mean renegotiating parental, household, and career roles. Sometimes, mobility, while challenging, can be the crucible in which families and family members can discover their own particular identities and roles and the way in which they shift over time.

In this passage, we can see a similar dynamic at work in the Holy Family's experience of migration. In Matthew's infancy narrative, Joseph is a central figure, perhaps *the* central figure, and he is shown to be a just and righteous man. Already, inspired by a message from an angel in a dream, Joseph had made the righteous decision to accept Mary into his home and recognize Jesus as his son (Matt 1:20-25). Now, after another dream, he makes the bold decision to lead his family into Egypt, and they become refugees.

It is through the experience of mobility that Joseph navigates not only where his family will go, but indeed how he will understand his own identity and his critical contributions to his family. Matthew's presentation of family roles amidst mobility might similarly resonate with us as we reflect on our own experience of family roles and decision-making.

Not only does this migration story help us see how Joseph practices righteousness within his family, it also helps us see how Joseph, Mary, and Jesus are living out, in their own particular way, *other* stories of righteousness, migration, and freedom embedded in Israel's history. As with Bethlehem (see *Setting the Scene*, above), so too the journey to Egypt becomes a way for Matthew to connect the Holy Family's particular story of migration with other scriptural stories that are part of their kinship and national identities. Thus, like Joseph in the book of Genesis (Gen 37ff.), so too Matthew's Joseph is given wisdom in dreams that result, despite the scheming of others, in finding refuge in Egypt. And just as Moses was saved from Pharaoh's massacre of the Hebrew boys (Exod 1 and 2), so too Jesus is saved from Herod's schemes. Like Moses, Jesus' story will be one of teaching and freedom for his people. Finally, Matthew applies the warm parent-child imagery of the prophet Hosea (11:1): Jesus, like the people of Israel, is cared for as God's son in the midst of migration. After his baptism, Jesus will again be identified as God's beloved son (Matt 3:17). Can we see ourselves as "beloved children" in our own

If you had to name your extended family's "story" in a word or a phrase (perhaps give it a "title"), what would it be? Why?

Would that word, phrase, or title also be a good descriptor for your own individual or household story today? Why or why not?

mobility, inseparable from our loving God and our families, even as we renegotiate our family roles and connection to our family stories?

16When Herod realized that he had been de-
ceived by the magi, he became furious. He or-
dered the massacre of all the boys in Bethlehem
and its vicinity two years old and under, in ac-
cordance with the time he had ascertained from
the magi.17Then was fulfilled what had been said
through Jeremiah the prophet:

18"A voice was heard in Ramah,
sobbing and loud lamentation;
Rachel weeping for her children,
and she would not be consoled,
since they were no more."

Have you had an experience of sharing family pain across great distance? What kind of impact did it have in your life and your family relationships?

This passage (and the prophetic quotation from Jeremiah 31:15) reflect an important mood prevalent at the beginning of Matthew's gospel: an impending darkness and danger, which is personified here by both Herod's brooding and Rachel's weeping. This danger is shown as being experienced and shared across great distance. In our mobility as families, we may also find ourselves sharing one another's burdens and despairs across great distance, as when we encounter illness, addiction, and death. Often, sharing family pain across distance can be another source of strain.

It is easy to get caught up in the various prophetic texts that Matthew quotes in his infancy narratives, seeing them either as evidence that the life of Jesus was foreseen by Israel's prophets (which was certainly not their original purpose) or as quotes around which Matthew constructed his narrative. Biblical scholar Raymond Brown, however, suggests a different approach: Matthew's infancy narrative could surely stand on its own without these quotations, and so their real purpose was as a teaching tool that helped Christians strengthen their faith by making connections between the Jesus story and Jewish biblical faith (*The Birth of the Messiah*). We would do well to reflect on how the passages might strengthen us as we live through family pain.

Rachel was the wife of the patriarch Jacob and viewed as the mother of the entire people—both of the kingdom of Israel in the north and Judah in the south. While there is some scholarly debate about the location of Ramah (nearer to Jerusalem or to Bethlehem for example), there can be no doubt that the weeping of Rachel is meant to evoke a sense of shared grief—across generations and across geographic landscapes. The tone of grief at the time of exile is being married to the situation in Bethlehem where Herod executed Israel's children.

In the midst of this shared grief, the Gospel of Matthew proclaims *Emmanuel, God is with us* in Jesus (Matt 1:23). Even if distanced from this massacre during his family's sojourn in Egypt, nevertheless Jesus' life story is intimately interwoven with it, and his presence remains in Bethlehem's pain. So too can we be present to one another as families, even across great distance. Sometimes, we may indeed be able to make concrete contributions that help alleviate one another's struggles. But more often, we may need to simply make room in our hearts to listen and lament, embracing the pain that is being encountered by family members in another part of the country or world.

What does it mean to you to be "present" to another family member's struggle, especially when you are living in another place?

19When Herod had died, behold, the angel of the
Lord appeared in a dream to Joseph in Egypt
20and said, "Rise, take the child and his mother
and go to the land of Israel, for those who sought
the child's life are dead." 21He rose, took the
child and his mother, and went to the land of
Israel. 22But when he heard that Archelaus was
ruling over Judea in place of his father Herod,
he was afraid to go back there.
And because he had been warned
in a dream, he departed for the
region of Galilee. 23He went and
dwelt in a town called Nazareth,
so that what had been spoken
through the prophets might be
fulfilled, "He shall be called a
Nazorean."

Matthew paints a picture of a particularly arduous journey to Nazareth for the holy family. Still leading his migrant family,

Joseph has one or more dreams that it is safe to return—but to settle his family in Galilee instead of Judea, so as to avoid Herod's son Archelaus. Historians tell us that upon the death of King Herod the Great, the Roman Empire divided Israel into three areas. His son Archelaus was indeed given the areas of Judea and Samaria for a short time, before being removed by Rome. Joseph decides to settle his family instead in Galilee, which was given to another son, Herod Antipas, the Herod who will appear later in the gospels. Like many migrants today, the Holy Family's personal settlement story mingles with much larger realities of politics, repression, and terror.

In a way, Joseph's decision to settle his family in Nazareth seems to be an accident of history. And yet, Matthew's creative use of prophetic texts also shows a confidence that Jesus truly *belongs* in Nazareth. Perhaps he is suggesting that, even if a "bud" (*nēser*) from the lineage of Jesse (David's father) (Isa 11:1), he will blossom in Nazareth. Or, perhaps he is suggesting that Jesus will not only be a Nazorean, from Nazareth, but also a Nazarite (*nāzîr*), consecrated to God (Num 6:1-21; Judg 13:2-7). Whatever Matthew's intention, this gospel text stretches our imagination, challenging us to discern God's presence in the midst of mobility—both our own and in the lives of so many migrants and refugees today. Moreover, we might reflect on how we and our families have come to "belong," wherever we live, and how we might help others to belong as well.

Did you move as a child? Or have you moved your family as an adult? What was it like "belonging" in new places?

The Holy Family settles, and Jesus is formed, in a particular village, Nazareth, in the shadow of the city of Sepphoris. While Sepphoris is clearly the more "important" location of the time, it is the village culture of Nazareth that shapes Jesus, and it is Nazareth, not Sepphoris, that is identified in the gospels. Perhaps we can relate to this type of "remembering": that we grew up in a particular town, or neighborhood, or block. Recent excavations in Nazareth suggest that it was a village of perhaps 50 households and 300 families, and the one family dwelling that has been discovered is a modest one. It was a place where people knew one another, so much so that when Jesus comes back after beginning his ministry, people remember him as the "carpenter's son" and have a hard time squaring their memory of him with the wisdom figure he has become (Matt 13:54).

What was life like in your childhood hometown(s)? How did it shape how you see life today? What is it like to return to your hometown?

Jesus and his family find a home in Nazareth, a place that nurtures who he is and who he will become. Neither Matthew nor Luke give us a fuller picture of his life there, except that it is a place where he grew in wisdom and strength (Luke 2:39). From his ministry and his later parables, we can detect images that may have been shaped by Nazareth village culture and his family's life there: images of farming (Matt 13:1-7) and building (Matt 7:24-27), family celebrations (Matt 25:1-13) and relationships (Matt 21:28-32).

However we have experienced mobility in family life, how have we (or our children) been shaped by the places we have called "home"?

When has an opportunity to help others settle in your neighborhood or church presented itself to you? How did you respond? Would you do anything differently upon reflection?

Praying the Word / Sacred Reading

God Abiding, world-igniting,
God of sun and moon and earth,
All our living, moving, being
Rests in you and finds it worth.

Though the storms of life may shake us,
And our hearts be filled with fear,
Still your peace lives deep within us,
And your promise always near.

God Abiding, hope surprising,
God of strength and tender might,
From the waters you have claimed us,
You have robed us with your light.

When we step into the darkness,
Ever faithful you remain.
You prepare a road of glory
Through despair and loss and pain.

Christ Abiding, Joy entwining
With our sorrow, grief, and loss.
In our grief we hear your groaning,
In our brokenness, your cross.

Help us heed prophetic voices,
Knowing you are in our midst.
May we comfort one another
Till your peace and justice kiss.

Living the Word

- *Families living mobility often draw strength from spiritual practices that connect them with their family. For example, some families have strong devotional practices (e.g., praying the rosary) or cultural practices related to popular religiosity (e.g., Día de los Muertos; Christmas oplatki; Simbang Gabi). If customs like this are part of your background, consider continuing to practice them. They are particular ways of experiencing God and community, and perhaps part of your family's connective tissue.*
- *At the same time, pay attention to new spiritual practices that might enrich you and your family's faith life. Perhaps your new parish has monthly Taizé Prayer or prays with musical styles that help you experience God in new ways.*
- *If you are distanced from extended family, be intentional (and realistic) about how you will stay in one another's lives: through visits, phone calls, and social media. Learn how to listen, learn, and lament with each other across distance.*
- *Consider ways you can be present to others who are experiencing their own migration or displacement: e.g., volunteering with agencies that teach English as a second language; helping children and families who are experiencing extended hospitalization; visiting those in prison or supporting families*

who are visiting incarcerated loved ones; and advocating for the rights and human dignity of migrants and refugees (see justiceforimmigrants.org or sharejourney.org, projects of the US Catholic Bishops, Catholic Relief Services, and Catholic Charities USA).

Mobility and Relationships

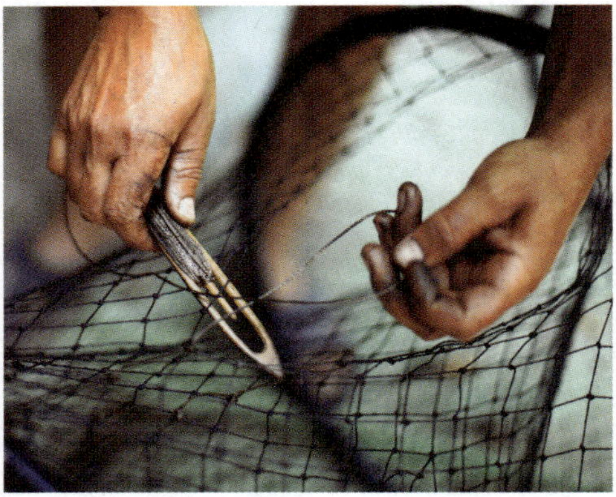

Pray for God to assist you in your prayer and study. Then read Matthew 4:12-25, which invites us to journey with Jesus and his earliest followers.

Matthew 4:12-25
12When he heard that John had been arrested, he withdrew to
Galilee. 13He left Nazareth and went to live in Capernaum by
the sea, in the region of Zebulun and Naphtali, 14that what
had been said through Isaiah the prophet might be fulfilled:

15"Land of Zebulun and land of Naphtali
the way to the sea, beyond the Jordan,
Galilee of the Gentiles,
16the people who sit in darkness
have seen a great light,
on those dwelling in a land overshadowed by death
light has arisen."

17From that time on, Jesus began to preach and say, "Repent,
for the kingdom of heaven is at hand."

[18]As he was walking by the Sea of Galilee, he
saw two brothers, Simon who is called Peter, and
his brother Andrew, casting a net into the sea;
they were fishermen. [19]He said to them, "Come
after me, and I will make you fishers of men."
[20]At once they left their nets and followed him.
[21]He walked along from there and saw two other
brothers, James, the son of Zebedee, and his
brother John. They were in a boat, with their
father Zebedee, mending their nets. He called
them, [22]and immediately they left their boat and
their father and followed him.
[23]He went around all of Galilee, teaching in
their synagogues, proclaiming the gospel of the
kingdom, and curing every disease and illness
among the people. [24]His fame spread to all of
Syria, and they brought to him all who were sick
with various diseases and racked with pain,
those who were possessed, lunatics, and para-
lytics, and he cured them. [25]And great crowds
from Galilee, the Decapolis, Jerusalem, and
Judea, and from beyond the Jordan followed him.

Consider some important background information as you begin to ponder the above passage from Scripture.

Setting the Scene

For those who are highly mobile, relationships are a particular challenge: is it possible to form meaningful friendships when one will only be in a place for a short amount of time? Will such friendships endure? Do they matter? We have already seen how Matthew's gospel tells the story of Jesus' infancy as one of migration, leading to his family's settlement in Nazareth. Here, with his entry into Capernaum, we are introduced to Jesus' extraordinarily mobile adult life. From Capernaum, he will walk in many places and touch the lives of diverse peoples—including the "great crowds" that will follow him (Matt 4:25). Jesus will experience mobility in an intrinsically relational way and yet with a dynamic that can be deeply challenging to us, as we shall see.

In between the infancy narratives and this passage, the Gospel of Matthew recounts how Jesus departed Nazareth and stepped into his adult wanderings: first, to the banks of the Jordan River (Matt 3:14; cf. Mark 1:9) in order to be baptized by John the Baptist; then, to the Judean desert, where Jesus experienced temptation (Matt 4:1-11); and finally, as this passage begins, by departing Nazareth for Capernaum and the Sea of Galilee (4:13).

Matthew (and the other gospel writers) have little to say about his childhood and upbringing in Nazareth, but many scholars suggest village culture would have had a strong imprint on Jesus' sense of identity. In the culture of his time, Jesus would have understood himself (and been understood by others) in a "socio-centric" or "dyadic" way, that is, always in relationship to his family, household, and village. Thus, for him to leave Nazareth would have been a significant rupture, which perhaps helps us to understand the cool reception he would receive when he returned

(13:54). Stepping away from Nazareth, did Jesus enter into other networks or relationships that helped him to move through his world? In our very different time and culture, how do we understand the networks and relationships that we experience as we move through *our* world?

By considering Jesus' experience as he approaches Capernaum, we can reflect on how we are shaped by the people who inhabit the various places we live, how we shape others, and how such relationships continue to have a formative impact on our vocation, wherever we may journey.

As you consider the meaning of this passage and how it relates to your life, continue to respond to the questions in a group discussion or in your own reflection.

Understanding the Scene Itself

**12When he heard that John had been arrested,
he withdrew to Galilee. 13He left Nazareth and
went to live in Capernaum by the sea, in the
region of Zebulun and Naphtali, 14that what had
been said through Isaiah the prophet might be
fulfilled:**

15"Land of Zebulun and land of Naphtali
the way to the sea, beyond the Jordan,
Galilee of the Gentiles,
16the people who sit in darkness
have seen a great light,

on those dwelling in a land overshadowed by
death
light has arisen."

[17]From that time on, Jesus began to preach and say, "Repent, for the kingdom of heaven is at hand."

Our selection begins with a reference to the arrest of John the Baptist (v. 12) and ends with Jesus proclaiming John's central message: "Repent, for the kingdom of heaven is at hand!" (v. 17; cf. Matt 3:2). This is a signal that in his earlier interaction with John (see *Setting the Scene*), Jesus encounters a person who will continue to be a reference point, and dialogue partner, for him later in life (cf. Matt 16:14). Indeed, the connection will evolve into two overlapping networks, not simply between these two individuals, but also their disciples. Lines of communication will emerge between the two movements so that Jesus and John the Baptist, even from afar, can continue to converse with and about each other (11:2-14; cf. 16:14ff.). Finally, when Jesus later hears of John's death, he will withdraw into a deserted boat to be by himself, perhaps in grief (14:1-12), just as he "withdraws" as this passage begins, upon hearing of John's arrest.

John the Baptist's influence in Jesus' life begins in a particular place—the Jordan River Valley—but then continues as Jesus moves on to new places. It happens at a particularly important time in Jesus' life—as he enters into his ministry—and then continues to be a source of identity later in his life's journey. Finally, it serves a particular vision—repentance and the kingdom of heaven—but one that Jesus will live out in his own way, demonstrating that the kingdom is present in Jesus in a way that John could scarcely imagine.

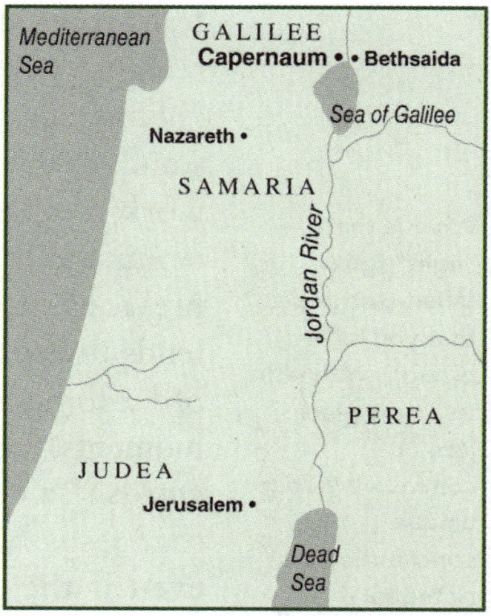

Anyone who has had a mentor can relate to this experience. Whatever our line of work, study, or particular skills, mentors are those who guide us in a particular time and place. Whether on campus, at a new job, or as we become parents, mentors teach, listen, support, strengthen, and challenge. A mentor is like a coach, attuned to our potential and pushing us beyond what we even thought possible, sometimes until we are out of breath. Often, they wear us out, but with the ultimate goal of building us up. At some point, we outgrow the time of mentorship and maybe even the place where we were mentored. Years and distance may grow between us and those who guided us, and we will also grow in new ways (even in ways our mentor may not recognize, just as John the Baptist had to question

Who has been a mentor(s) in your life? How do you continue to draw on their wisdom even today? How have you grown beyond the guidance they gave?

Jesus from afar). But the formative connection remains, wherever we go next.

What is the "light" (gifts, talents, attitudes) that you have brought with you to a new place, job, or community? Your unique contribution or potential contribution?

For Jesus, John's mentorship gives way as he stands at the threshold of a potentially new network of relationships, in a new place: Capernaum and the Sea of Galilee. As we saw in our previous discussion, the Gospel of Matthew tends to use prophetic texts in creative ways in order to highlight the significance of particular moments. Here, in 4:15-16, the prophet Isaiah's words (Isa 8:22–9:1) open our eyes to the light that Jesus brings as he enters this new place, even if the gospel writer may be confusing Capernaum with the very different location that Isaiah is referencing (Capernaum could be considered within the region of Naphtali, but not Zebulun). Nevertheless, this prophesy draws us into Jesus' journey as he moves "beyond the Jordan," beyond his experience with John the Baptist and into new encounters where he can be light for others.

18 As he was walking by the Sea of Galilee, he
saw two brothers, Simon who is called Peter, and
his brother Andrew, casting a net into the sea;
they were fishermen. 19 He said to them, "Come
after me, and I will make you fishers of men."
20 At once they left their nets and followed him.
21 He walked along from there and saw two other
brothers, James, the son of Zebedee, and his
brother John. They were in a boat, with their
father Zebedee, mending their nets. He called
them, 22 and immediately they left their boat and
their father and followed him.

In Jesus' time, Capernaum was a commercial center. It benefited from its position on an important trade route and the agricultural products that flowed from various places (including Jesus' home region around Nazareth). Most especially, Capernaum thrived due to the fishing industry on the Sea of Galilee and the ability to salt, preserve, and ship fish elsewhere. Perhaps Jesus was drawn there as a "carpenter's son," or as a skilled worker himself (Matt 13:55; cf. Mark 6:3), ready to participate in this economy by building and repairing boats or engaging in other construction projects. Nevertheless, recall again that, in moving on from Nazareth to this new place, Jesus would have been separating himself from a central part of his identity.

Whatever his reasons for arriving in Capernaum, once there he encounters men with a very different way of life than his own. Simon (Peter), Andrew, James, and John are fishermen, dependent on the trading economy that surrounds them. Moreover, just as Jesus' identity would have been rooted in his own family and hometown village culture of Nazareth, so too these men seem to be similarly tied to households in this region. Thus, we hear later in Matthew's gospel about Peter's home in Capernaum (Matt

8:14-15) and, right here in this passage, about the family business of James, John, and their father (v. 22).

As he stands on this Galilean shoreline and encounters the people of Capernaum, perhaps Jesus is overcome with the same emotions that touch us when we get to know a new community. Although we may feel out of place, the people we meet may very well be quite rooted. Although away from our own networks of family and friends, those around us may have lives deeply interwoven with *their* families and others they have known since childhood. The patterns of life, work, and family that are new to us may be taken for granted by our new neighbors. We may feel like outsiders in this new place.

When have you experienced yourself as an "outsider" in a new place, while others have been "rooted" in family and other relational networks? (If this has happened to you more than once, how would you compare the various experiences?)

Perhaps he is an outsider, but Jesus becomes an insider in the lives of these fishermen and changes them forever. By inviting them to "Come after me," he recognizes the significance of his journey's wisdom, not only for him, but also for them. He is not afraid to shake them up, alter their lifestyle, give their life "a new horizon and a decisive direction" (Pope Benedict XVI, *Deus Caritas Est* 217; quoted in Pope Francis, *Evangelii Gaudium* 7). In inviting them to follow him, Jesus boldly suggests that they too move beyond their own comfort zones. He calls them using their own language, their own fishing lingo, but in a way that stretches their imagination: "I will make you fishers of men." Remarkably, his presence and call really do transform them, and they follow him into the unknown.

Some scholars point to the particularly strong relationship Jesus will have with the four men named here, as well as his other closest disciples, and identify it as an example of "fictive kinship"—a kind of "chosen family" found in some movements of the time. This might seem unremarkable to us in the age of sitcoms like *Friends* or *How I Met Your Mother*, but in Jesus' sociocentric and household-oriented culture, as we have seen, it would have been extraordinary. Although initially an outsider, Jesus will later claim his disciples as family (Matt 12:49), and will share important "mountaintop moments" with these men in particular (Matt 7:1-8), as well as moments of honesty (Matt 20:20-24) and pain (Matt 26:46).

Although initially an outsider, Jesus will later claim his disciples as family.

Have we ever become "insiders" in the lives of those we encounter in a new place? Perhaps we have found ourselves learning, even internalizing, the customs, values, and "lingo" of our new homes, our new neighbors. At the same time, we may find that, in the midst of our mobility, we transform the lives of others in surprising ways.

[23]He went around all of Galilee, teaching in their
synagogues, proclaiming the gospel of the king-
dom, and curing every disease and illness among
the people. [24]His fame spread to all of Syria, and
they brought to him all who were sick with
various diseases and racked with pain, those

Have you ever moved from being an "outsider" to an "insider" in someone's life, deeply affecting them in ways that changed the ways they live their life, even their life's trajectory?

who were possessed, lunatics, and paralytics, and he cured them. [25]And great crowds from Galilee, the Decapolis, Jerusalem, and Judea, and from beyond the Jordan followed him.

Later in the Gospel of Matthew, Capernaum is referred to as Jesus' "own city" (Matt 9:1), perhaps a reflection of how formative his time there would be for both his relationships and later itinerant ministry. In our own itinerant lives, maybe we can also identify those places that were important "homes" for us, not because we grew up there, but because they were settings in which we formed important relationships and grew in new and surprising ways. For example, many young adults grow enormously during brief stints living in big cities, traveling to distant lands, or working in small towns in their own country. Those places will continue to hold a special place in their hearts for the rest of their lives.

In your own mobility, have you lived in a place that was "temporary" but where you discovered important things about yourself, your skills and passions?

Looking back, we might also remember our time in such as places as "hinge moments" in our lives, launching us toward new locales, career trajectories, and family experiences. With a large and diverse population that includes residents and traders from various surrounding regions, Capernaum launches Jesus, into a much larger network throughout Galilee (and then beyond), allowing him to share and live his vision about the kingdom of heaven. These verses summarize what Jesus' ministry will become beyond Capernaum: to proclaim the Gospel, especially through his teaching and healing ministry (vv. 23-25; see also Matt 9:35). It is in and

around Capernaum (8:5-17; 9:1-33) that Jesus begins this healing and teaching ministry, and the encounters he has there will have an enduring transformative effect on both him and many that he healed (e.g., Peter's mother-in-law, Matt 8:14-15). Capernaum gives Jesus the space to fully explore and expand aspects of his identity, skills, gifts, and passion. This is also an important practice for many young adults today. Perhaps adults of all ages may relate to the movement of coming into one's own.

Can you think of relationships from past places that were important in helping you become who you are?

Jesus' journeying through, and then beyond, Capernaum suggests a tension, one that might resonate with any who negotiate relationships, vocation, and mobility. On the one hand, many of the relationships that Jesus forms in and around Capernaum endure, including those with Peter, James, and John, and he clearly experiences success in his ministry there. On the other hand, he is not bound to Capernaum by rose-colored glasses: with stark words, he will later remember those who did not respond to his preaching in that city (Matt 11:23-24; Luke

10:15). Even more important, his experiences in and around Capernaum show him the great need that exists beyond its region, personified by the crowds from all over streaming to find him. Despite his obvious love for the city, despite the new network he has found there, he is called to embrace his teaching and healing ministry, wherever it may take him.

Like Jesus, indeed as followers of Jesus, we too may sometimes feel called to move beyond the comforts of place and relationship into the great needs of our world, embracing God's presence in our journeys, God's movement in our gifts. Amid this mobility, relationships may be stretched, and we may experience both joy and pain. Some relationships may well break while others flourish in surprising ways and new relationships spring forth as we encounter the great crowds in our journeys. By being attentive to the relationships we encounter in our mobility, we may find ourselves sometimes feeling nostalgic for the places we have left, missing those who are absent from our day-to-day-lives, or overwhelmed by new encounters. Nevertheless, by practicing gratitude for our relationships, we can appreciate how we have been shaped and how we have helped shape others, as we move from home to home.

Make a list of relationships that have been important to you in various places where you have lived, offering their names to God in gratitude.

Praying the Word / Sacred Reading

A journey invites, born of water and wilderness,
Dripping with freedom, and struggle, and prayer.
Our hearts long to follow, God's reign in our midst!
Called to the journey of Christ!

A soul-healing touch, for the scarred and the sorrowing,
Caressing with presence, making holy our pain.
Our suffering transformed as discipleship's dignity,
Renewed on the journey of Christ!

A vision that shatters all borders and boundaries,
Enlightening our eyes to lives torn by fear.
We hunger together, sharing death and new life,
Embracing the journey of Christ!

Living the Word

- *When moving into a new area and new parish, consider joining a small faith group. (Perhaps you are reflecting on this Alive in the Word volume as part of a small faith group!) You may find that there are a variety of small faith groups, including Bible studies, book studies, prayer groups, those that reflect on the Sunday Lectionary readings, and those part of a larger parish renewal program. Whatever small faith group you choose or find yourself in, it is a spiritual practice that can enliven your experience of*

God and community—even if you are only in a community for a short period of time.

- *Consider being a mentor for someone else—for example, through an organization like Big Brothers, Big Sisters, in your parish as a confirmation or marriage sponsor, at work (as appropriate), or through your college or high school's alumni network.*
- *Whatever your reason for mobility, see if you can maximize the opportunity to grow in surprising ways by trying out new activities. Perhaps you live in an area where you can try a pastime or sport completely new to you. Taste new types of food. Listen to new types of music. Move outside your comfort zone.*